Odell Beckham Jr.: The Inspiring Story of One of Football's Greatest Wide Receivers

An Unauthorized Biography

By: Clayton Geoffreys

Table of Contents

Foreword

Odell Beckham Jr. is easily one of the best wide receivers to ever play football. He has accomplished a lot in his young career. As recently as 2016, Beckham Jr. became the fastest player in NFL history to have recorded 200 career receptions along with 4,000 career receiving yards. This is no easy feat. Thank you for purchasing *Odell Beckham Jr.: The Inspiring Story of One of Football's Greatest Wide Receivers*. In this unauthorized biography, we will learn Odell Beckham Jr.'s incredible life story and impact on the game of football. Hope you enjoy and if you do, please do not forget to leave a review!

I read every review and your feedback helps inspire me to continue writing for you.

Also, check out my website at claytongeoffreys.com to join my exclusive list where I let you know about my latest books. To thank you for your purchase, you can go to my site to download a free copy of *33 Life*

Lessons: Success Principles, Career Advice & Habits of Successful People. In the book, you'll learn from some of the greatest thought leaders of different industries on what it takes to become successful and how to live a great life.

Cheers,

Clayton Geoffreys

Visit me at www.claytongeoffreys.com

Introduction

The world of American football is full of great personalities that each have their own special way of showing how unique they are on and off the pitch. After all, in such a competitive environment as the NFL, players need to have something of their own to make themselves stand out—regardless of whether or not we are talking about something positive.

Of course, what also makes a really good athlete a superstar is not only how he plays on the field and how he affects the way his team plays, but also how he carries himself as one of the more popular personalities, not only in the NFL but in the entire world of sports. The best NFL players usually play with the kind of competitive flair and edge that allows them to stay relevant in the league. There are also those whose personalities tend to stand out either in a positive or a negative way even when not playing the game. This is where Odell Beckham Jr. comes in.

Back in college, Odell Beckham Jr. was already one of the most prominent names in American football even though he had yet to play in the big leagues. The young man was already putting up good numbers in his freshman year with the LSU Tigers. During his junior year, he eventually went on to win one of the highest honors any collegiate player can ever hope to achieve, the Paul Hornung Award. As a wide receiver, you could hardly find a collegiate player as good as Odell Beckham Jr. was during his days with the LSU Tigers.

But, then again, Odell Beckham Jr. was not one of the more highly-touted players coming into the NFL when he was drafted third overall by the New York Giants during the 2014 Draft. He did not come in with the kind of flair and national attention that some of the other players had coming into 2014, as there were incoming NFL rookies considered to have more talent and upside than the 2013 Paul Hornung Award winner. And the worst part was, Beckham Jr. had to miss his first four weeks in the NFL because of a hamstring injury. He was not even able to make the most out of training camp and preseason due to his injury. In that regard, there were not a lot of expectations on the shoulders of the 12th overall pick of the 2014 NFL Draft.

Not many people realized that the New York Giants had a gem in their rookie wide receiver as they were heading into the season with a lineup depleted by injuries. In that regard, long-time quarterback Eli Manning did not have a lot of options to pass the ball to. The veteran was able to make do with what he had and allowed Odell Beckham Jr. to shine on the field as the main target of his passes.

Due to the depleted Giants lineup as well as Odell Beckham Jr.'s natural explosiveness, the young wide receiver was able to turn heads and become one of the most productive rookies of all time at his position. His production and his amazing (and surprising) first year in the NFL, despite missing the first four weeks of play, were enough to earn Beckham Jr. the Offensive Rookie of the Year Award for 2014.

But Odell Beckham Jr.'s career was only getting started. He began to pile up stats at a rapid pace due to his amazing productivity. It was in 2016 when the former LSU star became the fastest player in league history to reach 200 career receptions and 4,000 career receiving yards. That season was the first 100-reception season in his career as he helped the New York Giants reach the playoffs with a record of 11-5.

As good as Beckham Jr. has been on the field and on paper, there was always something about him that made him a bigger-than-life personality—far bigger than what he does on the field. He has seen his fair share of frustrating moments and has always been vocal about any problem he sees with how his team plays and uses him. Beckham Jr. is nothing short of talented in any way you look at his production, but his temper has gotten the best of him throughout his entire career. He has been regarded as "easily combustible". On top of that, he has also said a few controversial things that were either related to the way his team played or had something to do with things outside the realm of football.

Beckham Jr. became a popular athlete to many fans around the world largely due to how different he was in comparison to all the other players in the NFL. At a time when the league seemed a bit more formal than it was years ago, Odell Jr. was credited for being one of the few remaining "fun" guys in the entire NFL. His flamboyant and "childish" personality and his tendency to always find himself in the middle of a lot of controversy have allowed Beckham Jr. to rise as a player in a way that is larger than football itself. He became a fan favorite, but his overall personality also made him the target of attacks from the media and even some other NFL personalities.

In that regard, no matter how good Odell Beckham Jr. was on the field, he was always the subject of criticism, not only because he was not able to translate his productivity to wins but also because his losses were the main reasons why he often showed and voiced his frustration in and out of the game. On top of that, despite his status as one of the most electrifying wide receivers the league has seen in a while, Beckham Jr. seemed like he lacked the discipline and focus to get all the way to the top.

As an individual, there is no argument that Odell Beckham Jr. was indeed a phenomenal player for the New York Giants, but the Giants eventually saw things differently as they decided it was time to part ways with their star wide receiver. In March of 2019, he was traded to the Cleveland Browns where he got a fresh new start. Beckham Jr. was hoping to silence his critics as he continued to ascend as one of the top players at his position and in the entire NFL.

Chapter 1: Childhood and Early Life

Odell Beckham Jr. was born on November 5, 1992, in Baton Rouge, Louisiana. It was in Louisiana where the young Beckham Jr. emerged as a rising star. However, Beckham Jr. could thank his natural prodigious talent and physical gifts as an athlete for making it easier for him to rise up in the world of sports even when he was young.

Beckham Jr.'s father, Odell Sr., was an athlete himself. When he was young, Odell Sr. was a pretty good player and a productive running back for the LSU Tigers from 1989 to 1992. The elder Beckham ran a total of 757 yards and 152 carries during his days with the LSU Tigers.[i] Needless to say, Beckham Jr.'s father also had a respectable career as a football player after spending all four of his college seasons at LSU. The younger Odell even claims that his father was roommates with another LSU star, Shaquille O'Neal, who is regarded as one of the greatest and most dominant players in the history of the NBA.

Meanwhile, it was not a one-sided affair in the Beckham family when it came to sports. Odell Jr.'s mother, Heather Van Norman, was also a star athlete back in her prime. Heather spent her years with the LSU Tigers as a track and field runner.[i] She excelled primarily as a sprinter but she was pretty good in the jumping events as well.

Given that both of Odell Beckham Jr.'s parents were gifted athletes and well-trained in the art of running and sprinting, it was only natural that their child would inherit their genes as a gifted athlete himself. The combination of his father's pedigree as a running back and his mother's talent as a track star gave Beckham Jr. the natural giftedness he used as a springboard when he was still young. Of course, his body may have been naturally made to allow him to excel as an athlete, but Odell Jr. also inherited his parents' love for sports.

Odell Beckham Jr. grew up as a big fan of sports in general. He was a natural-born athlete who could not only do what most other athletes were able to do, but he was also a fan of all sports. And despite the fact that he lacked size, had the speed, coordination, skill and unwavering determination to excel in whichever sports realm he placed his focus on.

Odell Beckham Jr. made a name for himself as a young athlete on the rise in Louisiana. Surprisingly, he did not only excel in football. Odell Jr. was intent upon developing into a well-rounded athlete by playing almost all of the sports he had learned as a child. Football was always at the center of it all, but Beckham Jr. was just as gifted in basketball, track, and even soccer (the original football). He followed in his mother's footsteps as a track star and even went on to become a great sprinter and jumper.

Soccer was also an option for Odell Beckham Jr. In fact, as a child, he idolized soccer star David Beckham, whom he shares a family name with although they are no relation. When he was about 4 or 5 years old, he sometimes joked around that having the same family name with the soccer megastar was his only reason for playing soccer. Beckham Jr. has long been a fan of Beckham and was always clowning around that he was related to David.[ii]

Given all that, it was easy for Odell Beckham Jr. to find a way for himself in the world of sports. That child developed so well as an athlete that he immediately rose up to become a star in all the sports he played. His experience as a high-performance athlete in many different sports helped turn Beckham Jr. into the explosive and well-coordinated wide receiver he is today.

Chapter 2: High School Career

Odell Beckham Jr. spent his childhood years as a competitive multi-sport athlete, due to how he had inherited his parents' love for sports. He was not new to the life of an athlete and continued to be a competitive athlete when he began high school. He attended Isidore Newman School in New Orleans, which was about 81 miles away from his hometown of Baton Rouge. In his new school, Beckham Jr. lettered in three different sports—namely basketball, track, and football.

Isidore Newman is not an unknown school in the world of football. Archie Manning III, a capable quarterback himself back when he was still with the NFL, sent all three of his sons to Newman. Cooper Manning was not able to make a career out of football after being diagnosed with spinal stenosis at the age of 18. However, his other two sons, Peyton Manning and Eli Manning, turned out to be NFL quarterbacks worthy of the Hall of Fame. The youngest brother, Eli, would eventually be Odell Beckham Jr.'s quarterback while playing for the New York Giants. However, while Beckham Jr. was still trying to make a name for himself as a high school star, Peyton and Eli were already in the NFL and had put Newman on the map as two of the best athletes the school had ever seen. It was up to Odell to continue the legacy of fine Newman football players.

Back when he was in his younger years, Beckham Jr. was active in basketball, track, football, and soccer. He had a chance to continue playing soccer in high school, but he chose to forego that path in his formation as an all-around athlete. Odell had been pretty active in playing soccer up until that point, but there was a need for him to give it up when he was 14 years old because his youth coaches had wanted him to spend time training overseas. Thus, he could have been a national team soccer player but decided not to because the training in Europe would have prevented him from also training in all the other sports he loved back then.[iii] As such, there was a need for him to trim down his list of sports.

Basketball was another of the many sports that Odell Beckham Jr. was naturally gifted in. Growing up, he never had the size to be able to play the sport at its highest level. But then again, his athleticism was an entirely different story. Odell Sr. and Heather were both great athletes who could run hard and leap high. The combination of their genetics allowed Odell Jr. to excel in basketball, as he was faster and more explosive than anyone else on the floor despite his lack of height.

Standing about 5'7" throughout the earlier parts of his high school days, there was no reason at that time to believe that Odell Beckham Jr. was going to become a professional basketball player, yet he was still good enough to excel as a guard in high school and played all four years as a standout player for Isidore Newman.

He lettered all four years he played the sport as a prep athlete and eventually went on to be named one of the best basketball players in his district during his junior and senior years.

To this day, Odell Beckham Jr. still plays basketball during his free time and has indeed proven that he is freakishly athletic by performing ridiculous and contest-level dunks even though he stands shorter than six feet (and shorter than almost all of the point guards in the NBA). Had Beckham Jr. been a handful of inches taller, there is a big possibility that he would be playing basketball at the professional level instead of football.

Meanwhile, his continued training in track and field also allowed Odell Beckham Jr. to develop his speed, explosiveness, and coordination. He also spent all four years of his high school career as a letterman for Newman High in track and field. Odell Jr. loved track, his mother's own sport, and went on to perform at a star level in sprinting and jumping events. Back in 2010, he won second place in the Newman Invitational after measuring a leap distance of 6.83 meters. In the LA 2A State Meet that same year, he went on to record a leap of 6.71 meters in the long jump event and recorded a time of 22.31 seconds in the 200-meter dash event. He earned sixth place in both those categories and was obviously good enough to stand up against the best track and field athletes in the entire state of Louisiana.

However, even though Odell Beckham Jr. loved both basketball and track, his heart always belonged to football. He might have been excellent in all of the other sports he played because of how naturally gifted an athlete he was, but he was just freakishly good as a football player and could play multiple positions at any given time. He spent his high school years playing wide receiver, quarterback, running back, and cornerback because he had the skill and the athletic gifts to do so.

Even in the NFL today, Odell Beckham Jr. has shown flashes of stardom that hint at what might have been had he chosen to play the quarterback position. In practices later as a professional, he could throw the ball 40 to 70 yards with either hand. It was as if he was destined to play the quarterback position and become one of the greatest players to ever play the most important role in the sport. Back in high school, a simple decision to take the quarterback position for himself would have completely changed the way he developed in football. However, opting not to play quarterback in high school is one of the few unspoken, unselfish decisions he has ever made in his life.[iv]

For all his penchant for flair and his tendency to want to be under the spotlight later in his NFL career, Odell Beckham Jr. decided that he did not want to become the center of attention in his high school career when he made the choice to primarily play wide receiver instead of grabbing the quarterback role for his beloved Newman High School.

The decision to play wide receiver came about due to a very personal reason. Fellow Newman football player and Beckham's close friend, Ryan Brenner, grew up playing and developing in the sport together with Odell Jr. They played a lot of football together when they were in the eighth grade, where they were not able to win many games but were good enough together as a pair for Beckham to show his greatness as a potential quarterback. Almost all of the touchdowns the team scored through the air were due to Odell Beckham Jr.'s talents as a passer.[iv] He was already better than Brenner, even though the latter was the designated quarterback of their eighth-grade team.

However, Odell Beckham Jr. had known for a very long time that Ryan Brenner's dream was to eventually become Newman High School's primary quarterback. Brenner knew that Beckham Jr. was better than he was at that position, but Odell Jr. was just too special as a wide receiver. Other than the fact that Beckham was better off playing wide receiver than quarterback, he wholeheartedly believed that Brenner deserved to have the team's most important position, even though they both knew that Ryan was never going to attract a lot of attention from college scouts. For Ryan Brenner, Odell Beckham Jr. was always a player who wanted his teammates to get more attention than he did. He would rather make the decision that would allow the team to win instead of wanting to be the man under the spotlight.[iv]

Meanwhile, Beckham Jr.'s high school coach, Nelson Stewart, had the same opinion of his star high school player. At just 16 years old, Odell Jr. was already showing the kind of maturity and unselfishness of an older and more experienced player. All he cared about was what was on the scoreboard; winning was much more important than having the ball in his hands on every down. Of course, Odell also thought that his close friend was a great system player, he had great chemistry with him, and the team was better off with Brenner quarterbacking for Beckham.[iv]

While he played multiple positions in high school, Odell Beckham Jr. did indeed prove that both he and the team were better when he played wide receiver. He broke out of the gate during his junior year in 2010 when he scored a total of 10 touchdowns and caught 45 passes for a total of 743 yards. Then, as a senior, Beckham Jr. went on to have a total of 19 touchdowns and 50 catches for 1,010 yards to be named the district's Offensive MVP and the AA State Offensive MVP.

All of Odell Beckham Jr.'s accomplishments did not come so easily only due to his natural pedigree for the sport. Stewart said that he was one of the hardest working players he has ever coached in his entire career as the man leading the charge for Newman High School. The role of quarterback had always been the key for Newman because it was so used to running plays that relied on the strengths of great quarterbacks such as the Mannings. However, he did not have a Peyton or an Eli when Ryan Brenner was the one running plays for the team. Instead, his best player was the wide receiver named Odell Beckham Jr.

Looking at the strengths of his best player allowed Stewart to try to become more creative to accommodate what Beckham Jr. could do.[iv] He had to make the offense more suitable to the elite athletic abilities and innate feel that Odell had. In turn, Newman High School turned into a team that was more versatile and a lot faster than any of the squads led by either of the Mannings back in their day. And the best part was, Odell Jr. was not only a wide receiver, since there were moments when he had to do it all as the quarterback, the running back, and the cornerback.

Odell Beckham Jr. was so good that Stewart had to make an exception to one of his rules—he was allowed to perform a one-handed catch. In football, receivers are not advised to catch the ball with one hand because of the degree of difficulty in securing the catch with a single hand. But Stewart saw how effortless it was for his star wide receiver to perform one-handed catches because of the young man's supreme gifts. He was born with hops and a hangtime that are both reminiscent of what Michael Jordan could do in basketball. He could control his body well in midair and had the innate instinct to know when to explode for those catches. On top of that, he always had those freakishly long fingers that do not seem to be in proportion to the rest of his body. All that made it possible for Odell Jr. to perform feats that were almost impossible for any other player at his position. Stewart was forced to allow his best player to do the things only he could do.[v]

However, Odell Beckham Jr.'s greatness in all of the years he spent at Newman resulted from his hard work. Stewart said that he was watching films maniacally to study different plays and sets at a rate that was never ordinary for any teenager. After practices, they sometimes even had to turn the lights out because

Beckham Jr. just would not stop honing his game. This was the kind of player that any coach would certainly love to have, but would also be concerned about because of his crazy approach to perfecting his game. There was almost no rest for the young Odell Beckham Jr.

At the end of his senior year with Newman High School, Beckham Jr. ranked sixth nationwide as a wide receiver and 40th overall in the entire country. He obviously was one of the best players in the nation at that time and was rightfully getting a lot of attention from scouts from all of the most reputable college programs. The schools that were interested in him were LSU, Tulsa, Nebraska, and Ole Miss, among others.

Of course, there were a lot of reasons for college scouts to be so high on what Odell Beckham Jr. could do out there on the pitch. What scouts really loved about the young man was the explosive athleticism that more than made up for his stature as an undersized football player. It was an understatement to call Beckham Jr. a football player because he was simply an athlete who had the capacity and complete athletic tools to become one of the best in whatever sport he chose.

Then again, getting called an athlete in the world of football meant that Odell Beckham Jr. did not have an established role. Oftentimes, college scouts thought that he was just going to be a player that could play in whatever position needed his athleticism and explosiveness. That was why there were scouts who believed that he was eventually going to transition over to the cornerback position after spending a huge chunk of his high school career as a wide receiver.[vi]

But what scouts believed would make him excel as a wide receiver were his shiftiness and natural IQ. He may have already been freakishly fast, but he moved in a controlled manner that allowed him to shift speeds and changed directions in a heartbeat. He was not a racehorse that sprinted hard out of the gate without knowing how to pace himself. Rather, Odell Jr. was the jockey handling the reins of the racehorse because of how he was able to pace himself by using his natural feel and instincts, with or without the ball in his hands. Those qualities allowed Beckham to become one of the best targets for any quarterback during his high school years.

The entire recruitment process for Odell Beckham Jr.'s services started back in his junior year but did not end until his senior year. He did get a lot of attention from many schools but, at the end of the day, the top choices for him were LSU and Miami. It was during the early part of January 2011 when he made his decision public at the end of the third quarter of the US Army All-American Game. Because of his penchant for flamboyance, though but a very well-grounded athlete, he announced his choice by donning an LSU hat. It was obvious that he had chosen to go to LSU.

The decision to join the LSU Tigers was not a surprise. Not only was LSU one of the top recruitment programs in the entire country but it was also where he could trace his roots from. His father, Odell Sr., played for the Tigers during his prime days in college. Additionally, the younger Beckham's mother, Heather, was also a good athlete for LSU back in her time with the Tigers. Had Odell Sr. and Heather not chosen LSU, they would not have met one another. There would have been no Odell Beckham Jr. As such, Odell Jr.'s decision was also one rooted in legacy because it was important for him to follow in his parents' footsteps as LSU athletes.

When he signed with the LSU Tigers, he gave one of the simplest interviews anyone could expect of an athlete on the rise. The phrase "I'm going to work hard and make sure I'm ready" was what was most striking about his interview, as there was no arguing the fact that Odell Beckham Jr. was indeed ready to make a scene in the collegiate ranks regardless of how humble he was about how well prepared he was to play in a competitive scene that was totally different from the one he was accustomed to in high school.[vii]

For all of his accomplishments as a rising wide receiver, Odell Beckham Jr. had a reason to believe that he had to work harder than anyone else to make sure he would make the smoothest transition into the collegiate ranks. His good friend Ryan Brenner admitted that his buddy was always doubted back in high school. Though Beckham Jr. was consistently rated the top high school wide receiver in the entire state, critics were skeptical about what he could do at the college level because of his lack of size. Nevertheless, Brenner knew that all those criticisms were what fueled Odell Jr. to work harder than he had ever done. This allowed him to make a big splash in the college football scene, even after being doubted pretty much his entire career in high school.

Chapter 3: College Career

Odell Beckham Jr. entered LSU as a freshman player who did not have to redshirt or spend a year off, unlike other players. This was because the Tigers already believed that the freshman player was physically and mentally ready to take on the task ahead of him and to face challenges that were far more superior to that of the ones he had experienced back in his high school years.

Nevertheless, even though Odell Beckham Jr. was able to athletically and mentally adjust well to the collegiate ranks, there were not a lot of expectations on him for the very reason that he was recruited by the LSU Tigers at the same time as five-star recruit Jarvis Landry, the nation's fourth-best wide receiver. In that regard, the pressure and all eyes were on Landry to perform well at his position as a freshman. Meanwhile, there were not many people who thought that Beckham Jr. was ready to produce from the get-go.

But LSU Tigers head coach Les Miles thought differently of his prized freshman. He saw that Odell Beckham Jr. was always a hard worker and that he was willing to do the things the team was asking him to do while giving his best effort at doing so.[viii] That was the image that Beckham Jr. had built up ever since he was a high school star. The naturally-gifted athlete was one of those players a coach could always expect to work hard in practice, day in and day out, and who would always do more than what was asked of him just to get that win.

For Les Miles, there was nothing negative about his incoming freshman. Beckham Jr. was always about the team and was never going to do anything that was beyond what the team needed to get those wins. This image and reputation helped Odell Beckham Jr. turn into one of his coach's favorite players coming into his first season with the LSU Tigers. Of course, it also helped that he was coming into the team with the tremendous abilities he was gifted with and had worked so hard to hone and improve ever since his high school years.

What was questionable about Odell Beckham Jr. entering his first collegiate season was that there was never a certainty as to what position he was best-suited for. He was always a wide receiver who could play multiple positions back when he was in high school. However, it was also widely believed that he was too small for that position. Many thought he was going to be better off as a cornerback due to his height and his athleticism. In fact, Les Miles thought as much, too.

The LSU head coach at that time thought Odell Beckham Jr. was going to be useful to play a slot wherever it suited his skills. But what he noticed over time was that his freshman was getting bigger and stronger as he aged.[ix] He was always someone who had good feet and coordination on top of the athletic gifts he was born with. Additionally, he retained all the tremendous skills and physical attributes that scouts had raved about while getting bigger and stronger in the process. As Miles put it, you would not believe what Beckham Jr. could do if he just stood together with his teammates. You have to see him perform a catch to realize just how tremendous his ability is.

Fans of college football immediately saw what Odell Beckham Jr. could do once he suited up for the LSU Tigers. On September 3, 2011, he did not have the best first game in his collegiate debut with 2 receptions for 10 yards, but he more than made up for it the next game in a win over Northwestern State. In that game, Beckham Jr. had 5 receptions for 40 yards.

It did not take long for the freshman Odell Beckham Jr. to go for the first touchdown of his collegiate career. It was in his fourth game, which was against West Virginia on September 24th, when Beckham Jr. scored a touchdown after a 52-yard reception. Overall, in that game, the freshman had 2 receptions on 82 yards. A week after that, he went for another touchdown against

Kentucky. He had 3 receptions for 75 yards while scoring a touchdown in one of those receptions.

Odell Beckham Jr. did not have another touchdown from that point on until the end of the season. However, he always had at least 2 catches for a total of 36 receptions on 437 yards, or a total average of 12.1 yards in his first 11 games of the season. Those performances were enough for him to help the LSU Tigers win their first 11 games of the season. But during the 2011 SEC Championship Game against the Georgia Bulldogs, Odell Jr. showed signs that he was still indeed a young player finding his way in the collegiate ranks. Georgia held him to zero receptions in that matchup, although he did help enough for the LSU Tigers to win and reach the BCS Nationals, wherein they lost to the Alabama Crimson tide in a 21-0 game.

At the end of his first season with the LSU Tigers, Odell Beckham Jr. showed signs of stardom as he totaled 41 receptions for 475 yards and 2 touchdowns in the entire campaign. He was named to the All-SEC Freshman Team due to his marvelous first-year performance as a wide receiver for the Tigers, even after there were doubts about whether or not he could play that position at the collegiate level.

Coming into his sophomore year in college, Beckham had an increased role for the LSU Tigers as he started all but one of the 13 games he played that season. He immediately made some noise in just his first game of the regular-season campaign on September 1, 2012, against North Texas. In that season-opener, Odell Jr. had his first-ever punt return touchdown. He also finished that win with 3 receptions for 30 yards. Beckham then spent the next three games with a total of 8 receptions for 128 yards. But he eventually eclipsed those yard totals in one single game.

Against Towson on September 29th, Odell Beckham Jr. had his first-ever 100-yard game after finishing a win with 5 receptions and 128 yards, which was the total he had in his previous three games. He also finished that game with 2 touchdowns. However, the Tigers suffered their first loss of the season a week after that terrific performance against Towson. Beckham Jr. finished with 4 receptions for 78 yards in that defeat at the hands of Florida.

On November 17th, Odell Beckham Jr. had a relatively quiet game when LSU's rivals, Ole Miss, held him to just 2 receptions for a 13-yard total. However, he was clutch in that game even though he was struggling. It was the 89-yard punt return touchdown he had in the fourth quarter that helped tie the game for the LSU Tigers. His team eventually went on to beat their SEC rivals thanks to the pivotal performance by their sophomore wide receiver in the late portion of that tough game.

Against Arkansas a week after beating Ole Miss, Odell Beckham Jr. finished with his second 100-yard game.

He helped his team win by going for 4 receptions for 112 yards. But, in the 13th game of the season, the LSU Tigers ended up losing to Clemson. Odell Jr. had 3 receptions for a total of 40 yards in the second loss he suffered that year.

Finishing his sophomore year looking like he was a lot better than his freshman version, Odell Beckham Jr. had 43 receptions while leading the LSU Tigers for 713 yards. Needless to say, he was beginning to show signs of how good he truly was as an option for quarterbacks because of his combination of amazing speed, explosiveness, and timely catches.

It was during his junior season with the LSU Tigers when Odell Beckham Jr. formed one of the nation's deadliest receiving duos with fellow wide receiver Jarvis Landry. And thanks to the strong arm of their senior quarterback, Zach Mettenberger, the two receivers found it easier to display their extraordinary combination of athleticism and timing in what was a pro-style attack for the LSU Tigers. But what was really remarkable was that the duo showed how adept they already were at making even the most difficult catches. Both Beckham and Landry made fans roar with the one-handed catches that Odell Jr. had already mastered back when he was in high school.

As good as that duo already was at that point, Odell Beckham Jr. also made that year his breakout season. He started out that season by going for 5 receptions on a 118-yard total in a nationally-televised game against Texas Christian University. After that, he had his first back-to-back 100-yard games when he finished a win over Alabama-Birmingham on September 7th with 136 yards on a five-reception performance. On top of setting a new career-high in yards for a single game, Odell Jr. also finished with a career-high of 3 touchdowns in that amazing performance for one of college football's finest wide receivers.

Against Kent State on September 14th, Odell Beckham Jr. failed to make it three straight 100-yard games, but he did score a touchdown that game on 5 receptions for 76 yards. It did not take long for him to go for another 100-yard game as he finished a loss to Georgia with 118 yards and a total of 6 receptions.

Odell Beckham Jr. continued to shatter personal records as the season progressed. Against Mississippi State on October 5th, he went for a new career high in yards after going for 179 on 9 total receptions and 2 touchdowns in that win for the LSU Tigers. Three weeks after that amazing career performance, Odell Jr. went on to have the game of his collegiate career. In a win over Furman on October 26th, Odell Beckham Jr. made mincemeat out of their opponent's defense and went for a 204-yard total on only 6 receptions and 2 touchdowns.

While Odell Beckham Jr. was not able to replicate such a performance for the remainder of the season, he finished his most productive collegiate season yet. Odell Jr. finished second to Landry in both receptions and yards at 59 and 1,152 respectively. However, he was better in receiving yards per reception after finishing with a 19.5, as opposed to Landry's 15.5 average. Beckham also finished with 8 touchdowns behind Landry's 10.

The one thing that proved Odell Beckham Jr. was LSU's best player despite finishing second to Jarvis Landry in receptions, yards, and touchdowns was his versatility. He led the team in kickoff returns with 32 and kickoff yard returns with 845. No other player on the team even had more than 2 kickoff returns and 45 kickoff yard returns. He also had 18 punt returns on a total of 160 yards, proving that he was already a versatile force as a wide receiver at that point in his career. In fact, he even broke the LSU record of all-purpose yardage with a total of 2,315 yards. That helped cement his legitimacy as a member of the All-SEC First Team and the All-American Third Team.

Due to his amazing versatility in receiving and returning, Odell Beckham Jr. took the entire collegiate ranks by storm and went on to win the Paul Hornung Award at the end of his junior season in 2013. The award is given annually to the player regarded as the most versatile in all of college. That said, while Jarvis Landry may have been the slightly better wide receiver, Odell Beckham Jr. was miles ahead in all the other aspects needed for a team to win.

After such a tremendous junior season, Odell Beckham Jr. realized that his stock was as high as it could ever be, especially after winning a major award. That prompted him to make the decision to forego his senior year in college and try his luck in the 2014 NFL Draft. Done with college football and having proved that he was indeed good enough to stand on his own and even dominate the collegiate ranks, Beckham was on his way to a tougher competitive field in his quest to become a professional football player, a dream his father was never able to accomplish.

Chapter 4: NFL Career

Getting Drafted

Odell Beckham Jr. joined the 2014 NFL Draft as one of the big names that season thanks to the tremendous performance he had with the LSU Tigers in his junior year of college. However, as good as he was at LSU, there were other wide receivers that performed better than him at the collegiate level. As such, just like when he was in high school and about to enter college, there were not high expectations for Beckham coming into the NFL Draft. But that did not stop scouts and analysts from looking at his abilities using a more objective point of view.

Odell Beckham Jr.'s NFL Draft Combine performance was the first thing that the scouts and analysts needed to look at to make sure that they could come up with a more objective analysis of what the LSU star could do at his position and in comparison to the rest of the young football hopefuls vying for a spot for a team in America's premier professional sports league.

In terms of his physical measurements, there was nothing about Odell Beckham Jr. that actually stood out. He stands barely six feet tall and is shorter than the average NFL wide receiver height of 6'1". Considered undersized when he was in college, there was no question that he was coming into the draft as one of the shorter wide receivers.

However, to make up for his lack of height, Odell Beckham Jr. had some other impressive physical attributes. He may not look like a big man, but he does have a chiseled and strong body that is pure lean muscle at 198 pounds. Meanwhile, he also came into the draft with arms that are longer than any other person of his size. He was measured to have arms that are a quarter of an inch short of 33 inches. In comparison to the other standout wide receivers in college, Beckham Jr. has longer arms than the 6'1"

Sammy Watkins and only two inches shorter than the 6'5" Mike Evans.

But what was more impressive than Odell Jr.'s arm length was the size of his hands. While he may be shorter than the conventional wide receiver, he has hands that have allowed him to do the one thing that a wide receiver should do—receive the ball. His 10-inch hands allowed him to perform well in that department and made it look easy for him to perform those patented one-handed catches he was known for back in high school and college. In comparison, the taller Sammy Watkins and Mike Evans have hands that are a fraction of an inch shorter than 10 inches. With all due respect to Odell Beckham Jr., there is no arguing the fact that he has freakishly long arms and hands that have allowed him to make up for his lack of size out there on the field.

Athletic abilities were also some of the things that scouts looked at when they were analyzing what Odell

Beckham Jr. could do. He finished the 40-yard dash in just 4.43 seconds, the 10-yard split in 1.57 seconds, the 20-yard split in 2.58 seconds, the 20-yard shuttle in 3.94 seconds, and the three-cone drill in 6.69 seconds. He was also measured to have a vertical jump of 38.5 inches and a standing long jump of 10.2 feet.[x] In comparison to the two highly-touted wide receivers that were considered to be better than him, Beckham Jr. came out with the more impressive combine workout as far as his overall athletic abilities were concerned.

All that considered, there was no denying that Odell Beckham Jr. was coming into the NFL Draft as one of the more athletically-gifted wide receivers of that class. He may have been one of the shorter guys at his position, but his overall athletic talents were unquestionably impressive when you compared him to the other standout wide receivers vying for a slot in an NFL team.

Looking at his overall physical tools and athleticism, any scout could safely say that Odell Beckham Jr. had what it took to become a good wide receiver despite his height. However, analysts are also required to look at other factors and intangibles that are beyond what the measurements and the statistics might suggest.

For one, many lauded how Odell Jr. had the body and the willingness to get physical against defenders that were bigger than he was.[x] He may not have been tall, but his body was built for the increased physicality of the NFL. Beckham showed that he was never afraid of contact and, by making use of his explosiveness, he was strong enough to take and break tackles. He skillfully used his body and his broad shoulders to dive into defenders for extra yards.

As well built as Odell Beckham Jr. is, he also moves with a control and grace you might not expect from someone as chiseled as he is. He can easily shift his movements in the open field and has the ability to change direction in a heartbeat. His change-of-direction is at a level that makes it difficult for defenders to corral him even when he is going at full speed. And, on top of that, the quick feet he developed as a soccer player during his younger days allow him to beat presses but still make it possible for him to accelerate to full speed after maneuvering his way out of his defenders' coverage.

Odell Beckham Jr. is also excellent at controlling his body after the catch.[xi] The moment he makes a catch, he is so good with the ball in his hands that his overall combination of quick feet, athleticism, and IQ allow him to avoid even the best defenders on his way to earn some yards. As long as he has enough space, he will more than likely be good enough to make his tacklers miss. Also, because of this innate skill, he is so good at returning the ball that he has become one of the better return men at the wide receiver position. And when releasing the ball, Odell Jr. has shown how adept he is at using his quick burst of speed and explosive feet to get himself away from coverage.

It seemed as if LSU did indeed know how to utilize Odell Beckham Jr.'s physical gifts when they ran a pro-style offense that allowed the upstart wide receiver to run deeper routes than most other receivers at the college level. His ability to run so effortlessly and smoothly made it possible for him to fool the defense in his routes.[xi] In that regard, he would be able to adjust well to a similar style of offense often played at the professional level.

Terrific at making one-handed catches, Odell Beckham Jr. has shown that his height is indeed just a mere number that does not matter in the bigger scheme of things. His ability to go up for a ball using his superb vertical leap and his huge hands have allowed him to make catches that seem impossible for most people his size. He has consistently impressed crowds since high school with his patented one-handed catches. And while the NFL is an entirely different playing field, there was still a reason to believe that he could pull off such maneuvers because quarterbacks at the professional level are a lot more gifted than the ones Beckham Jr. had to play with since high school.

As far as his intangibles are concerned, there is no argument that Odell Beckham Jr. has an IQ that enables him to excel on and off the field. He has always been one of the more intelligent players in all the teams he played for thanks to his innate giftedness as a natural-born athlete and his hard work when it comes to studying plays during his free time. On top of that, he has always had the respect of his teammates because of how amazingly hardworking and competitive he is. Beckham will always be the first and last person off the practice field because of how maniacal his approach is at honing his craft. This can be clearly seen in how he was able to improve every year since entering college.

But, just like any other young athlete looking to make an NFL team spot, there were still things that held Odell Beckham Jr. back. For one, he was regarded as too short for his spot. Most wide receivers in the NFL are at least 6'1". In comparison, the highly-touted Texas A&M wide receiver Mike Evans stood at about 6'5" entering the draft. While Beckham may have had the physical tools that allowed him to make up for his lack of height, the consensus was that he was still too short to become a star wide receiver. This may be the reason why he was unable to make a lot of contested catches when he was playing for the Tigers.

When he is met by cornerbacks that are comparable to him in terms of speed, Odell Beckham Jr. struggles to get away from his defenders, as his speed is usually his best weapon out in the open field. This is evident when he tries to get over the top of the defense against cornerbacks that are just as fast or faster than him. In the NFL, it was more than likely he would meet defenders that are faster than those he came up against in college.

While Odell Beckham Jr. may have scored well in the 40-yard dash during the NFL Combine, he was not able to truly showcase his amazing speed in an actual game. Many considered that his playing speed was above average at best in comparison to receivers who also made it a point to play fast. This lack of elite-level speed was what scouts thought would prevent him from being an option as a slot receiver as he struggled to get over the top of the defense.[x]

But while Odell Beckham Jr. had a few chinks in his armor heading into the NFL Draft, he still had the physical tools and athletic gifts that allowed him to become a standout athlete at the wide receiver position. Nevertheless, there were reasons to believe that he was not the best at his position due to how the bigger Sammy Watkins and Mike Evans were physically more capable and had better collegiate careers than he did.

Come the day of the draft, Odell Beckham Jr., who was projected to be a mid-to-late first-round draft choice, was selected by the New York Giants with the 12th overall pick of the draft. He technically exceeded expectations, possibly because the Giants realized that they needed the best wide receiver available heading into the 2014 season.

Odell Beckham Jr. was the third wide receiver chosen in his draft class and was selected behind Sammy Watkins and Mike Evans. Nevertheless, after what had transpired in his rookie year all the way to the present, it is safe to say that Beckham was the steal of the draft and has also arguably become the best wide receiver not only in his class but perhaps in the entire NFL.

Offensive Rookie of the Year

While there were reasons to believe that Odell Beckham Jr. was going to have a productive rookie year with the New York Giants even after dropping to the 12th spot in the draft, problems struck as quick as lightning. A hamstring issue surfaced right before the season started and the injury forced Beckham to miss the majority of his first training camp as a professional football player. He also had to miss the first four weeks of the regular season because of his injury.

While he was still trying to recover from his injury, Odell Beckham Jr. watched the first four games of the New York Giants as quarterback Eli Manning, who he shares his Newman and Louisiana roots, struggled to find targets that could consistently catch the ball as well as he could back when he was still in college. Reliable wide receiver Victor Cruz and steady running back Rashad Jennings were both out due to injuries of their own. To that end, the star quarterback was passing the ball to role guys Preston Parker and Rueben Randle, who are not the most reliable guys at the receiver position, to say the least.[xii]

Seeing his team struggling without reliable receivers on any given night was the motivation that Beckham Jr. needed to keep him aching to get back on the field. No one was going to expect the 12th overall pick of the 2014 NFL Draft to have as much of an impact as the active receivers the New York Giants already had in their lineup. But Beckham Jr. was about to exceed the expectations the rest of the world had of him.

The moment Odell Beckham Jr. made his return, in the fifth week of the 2014 NFL season, things began to change for him and his entire team. In a game against the Atlanta Falcons on October 5, 2014, Beckham did not disappoint his team and made sure that all expectations set for him were broken. He made the play that sure enough made his debut a memorable one for him. Odell Jr. made a 15-yard touchdown catch from Eli Manning even though he was not open in the play. Upon seeing Manning releasing the ball and trusting the rookie that he would be able to finish the play, the man called ODB or OBJ used every bit of his explosiveness to get in front of the single-coverage defense and make a leaping catch that eventually was enough to give the Giants the win they needed in what was a struggling season for them.

Odell Beckham Jr. finished that game with 4 receptions on 5 targets for a total of 44 yards and 1 touchdown. He scored his first-ever touchdown at the professional level in his first game in the NFL right after coming back from a hamstring injury that hampered him. He might not have had the flashiest debut, but he made the right plays at the right time to prove that he was not just more substance than style. Since then, ODB made sure that he was not a one-hit wonder or a forgotten man that the defense just took it easy on in his first game.

While Beckham did not have the best performances in the losses to the Philadelphia Eagles and the Dallas Cowboys in Weeks 6 and 7, he made sure to have one of the best performances a rookie can have in his first taste of Monday Night Football in Week 9 against the Indianapolis Colts.

It was in that game against the Colts where Odell Beckham Jr. finished with his first 100-yard game as a professional football player. Though it came at a loss, he had 8 receptions for a total of 156 yards and a catch rate of 72.7%. He was indeed the receiver that Eli Manning and the New York Giants had been missing during the first four weeks of the season. Even with fellow wide receiver Cruz back on the field, Beckham was still the best target for Manning. To that end, the Giants made a huge switch in the way they played—Odell Jr. became the center of their offense.

Following that 156-yard performance against the Indiana Colts, Beckham Jr. followed up with 108 yards on 7 receptions out of 9 targets in the loss to the Seattle Seahawks on Week 10, just a few days after the rising star turned 22 years old. After a 93-yard performance in a loss to the San Francisco 49ers,

Beckham Jr. had a spectacular outing against the Cowboys on Week 11. He finished that game against Dallas with a 91% catch rate after making 10 receptions out of 11 pass targets. Beckham also had a total of 146 yards and 2 touchdowns in that game. However, it was his patented one-handed catch that truly caught the attention of the sporting world.

Odell Beckham Jr. made a one-handed touchdown catch that was so beautiful and so artistically done that writers all over the country hailed it as the "catch of the year". The catch transpired during the first play of the second quarter when Odell Jr. saw single coverage against cornerback Brandon Carr. Getting in front of Carr after he saw the release from the quarterback, ODB fought hard against his defender and was seemingly falling on his back when he rose up to make the catch. He had to stretch his right arm as far back as his shoulder could go while extending his fingers to their limit to make the touchdown catch. And as the slow-motion replay showed, Odell Beckham Jr.

needed only three fingers to make that catch. It was lauded as one of the most spectacular catches in the history of the sport by guys such as LeBron James, Kirk Morrison, and Victor Cruz.[xiii]

On top of that astounding catch by one of the most amazing rookie wide receivers in the game, Odell Beckham Jr. became one of only ten players in the history of the NFL since 1960 to record 8 receptions, 125 yards, and 2 touchdowns in an entire game. Even more impressively, he did that in the first half of that game against the Dallas Cowboys alone. But the Giants eventually crumbled in the second half of that game after momentarily losing Eli manning to an injury and ceding a game-winning touchdown to Dez Bryant with 61 seconds left on the clock.

Odell Beckham Jr. ended the month of November with one of the most spectacular numbers a rookie could have. He totaled for 38 receptions, 593 yards, and 2 touchdowns in that calendar month alone. Moreover, he had at least 90 yards in all of the games he played in November to put his name in the history books as the only NFL rookie to ever complete such a feat in a single calendar month.[xiv] In the middle of all of that, he also broke a rookie record for most consecutive games of at least 90 receiving yards in a single season. It took the end of the season for that record to stop as Beckham Jr. recorded at least 130 yards from then on until the conclusion of his rookie year.

If Odell Beckham Jr.'s November was already impressive, his December trumped what he had previously done. In a win over Tennessee on December 7th, ODB went for 11 receptions for 130 yards and a touchdown. He followed that up by going for 12 receptions out of 15 pass targets for 143 yards and a new career-high of 3 touchdowns in a win over the Washington Redskins on Week 15. With the 12 catches he had in that game, he tied a Giants rookie record once solely held by Mark Bavaro since 1985.

Against the St. Louis Rams on December 21st, Odell Beckham Jr. went for 8 receptions for 148 yards in a win for the New York Giants. He then ended his rookie campaign with a total of 12 receptions for 185 yards in a loss to the Philadelphia Eagles in the final week of the NFL regular season. It was clear that the Giants were looking for him in every play as he was the target of 21 passes the entire game.

Because of that performance, Odell Beckham Jr. broke the record held by Mark Bavaro. His 185 yards as a rookie were the most that a Giants player had ever had since Bavaro had 176 back in 1985. He also went on to tie Torry Holt's record for most games of 10+ receptions, 100+ yards, and at least 1 touchdown in a single season. The most impressive part of it all was that Odell Beckham Jr. was doing that as a rookie when no one had expected him to be as stellar as he was.

At the end of the regular season, Odell Beckham Jr. had a total of 91 receptions out of 130 pass targets, 1,305 yards, and 12 touchdowns. He became only the fourth rookie in league history to have at least 1,300 receiving yards in his first year in the NFL. On top of that, he also became the only rookie in the history of American professional football to have at least 90 receptions and 10 or more receiving touchdowns in a single year. And what made that even more incredible was the fact that Beckham had missed the first four weeks of play that season.

Because of his exceptional play all season long and the way he captivated fans and professionals alike with his astonishing catches, Odell Beckham Jr. was named a first-alternate for the 2015 Pro Bowl and was the injury replacement for Calvin Johnson. He effectively became the first wide receiver in the history of the franchise and the first Giants rookie in 13 years to make it to the Pro Bowl.

At the conclusion of the season, Odell Beckham Jr. became the obvious choice for many rookie awards. Many writers were describing his season as one of the best rookie campaigns in the history of the sport. He was named the Offensive Rookie of the Year by both the Associated Press and the Pro Football Writers Association.

His rookie season alone was enough for Odell Beckham Jr. to exceed all expectations and to erase all doubts about him coming into the NFL. The man once regarded as too short or not quick enough became one of the brightest young stars the league had seen in a long while. And he did that even though he was plagued by two hamstring injuries. A combination of skill, competitiveness, hard work, and overall athletic giftedness, Odell Beckham Jr. was a one-of-a-kind rookie for the New York Giants as he effectively became the center of the team's offense and their most important player outside of quarterback Eli Manning.

Not Slowing Down, No Sophomore Slump for OBJ

In any professional sport played, there will be times when a rookie stands out in the pack as one of the best first-year players to have played the game in a very long time. Sometimes, these are the players who were least expected to perform as well as they did due to various reasons that include low placement in the draft as well as the mistakes in judgment that scouts made when they evaluated such players. Oftentimes, the rookie may end up standing out because opposing defenses are not as keen or focused on stopping him because of a lack of scouting or preparation on their part. There will also be times when such a player plays well only because he is on a team with nothing to lose and with no other player capable enough to perform well.

All that considered, could someone possibly say that Odell Beckham Jr.'s rookie year was a mere fluke?

Was he only able to perform so well because opposing teams did not expect a lot from him? Or was he just able to put up all those fantastic numbers because the Giants had no other reliable player to catch the ball and they were force-feeding OBJ in a lot of those plays? Well, Odell Beckham Jr. would go on to answer all those questions in his second year in the NFL and would prove to the world that the sophomore slump did not apply to him.

Playing the season opener for the New York Giants for the first time in his career, Odell Beckham Jr. performed well against the Dallas Cowboys on September 13, 2015. The Giants suffered a narrow loss to the Cowboys in a game that saw ODB with 5 receptions for 44 yards. The following week, he bounced back well when he went for 7 receptions for 146 yards on a single touchdown in a loss to the Atlanta Falcons.

Beckham and the New York Giants got their first taste of victory that season against the Washington Redskins in Week 3. Odell Jr. finished with 7 receptions out of 9 pass targets for 79 yards and 1 touchdown. The team had a consecutive win a week later when they defeated the Buffalo Bills in what was a modest game for Beckham. He had just 5 receptions for 38 yards in that contest.

On October 11th, Odell Beckham Jr. bounced back to get his second 100-yard game of the season. In that win over the San Francisco 49ers, the rising sophomore wide receiver had 7 receptions for 121 yards and 1 touchdown. In a disappointing loss to the Philadelphia Eagles a week later, he scored his team's only touchdown after going for 7 receptions for 61 yards.

Through the first seven weeks of NFL play, Odell Beckham Jr. looked like he was in the middle of the dreaded sophomore slump as he only had two 100-

yard games while tallying a total of 42 receptions for 524 yards in those seven contests. That seemed too mediocre for a player who had finished his rookie season as strongly as he did the previous year. But that changed in the Giants' game against the New Orleans Saints, a shootout in front of the crowd that Odell Beckham Jr. had played for in his high school days.

In that 52-49 loss for the New York Giants in Week 8, Odell Beckham Jr. was responsible for 3 touchdowns after catching 8 of the 9 target passes he received for a total of 130 yards. That was the start of what was going to be a six-game streak of at least 100 yards for ODJ, who seemingly had just broken out of his brief sophomore slump.

Right after that game against the New Orleans Saints, Odell Beckham Jr. went for 9 receptions and became the target of 17 passes for a total of 105 yards. He may have struggled to catch the ball against the undefeated New England Patriots on Week 10, but OBJ still finished with 104 yards for 1 touchdown. In Week 12, he had 142 yards and 1 touchdown after catching the ball 9 times out of 18 target passes. He followed that up with 149 yards in an overtime loss to the New York Jets on December 6th. Odell Jr. had one of his better performances that season in a win over the Miami Dolphins on Week 14. He finished that game with 7 receptions for a season-high of 166 yards and 2 touchdowns.

After six straight games of at least 100 yards, Odell Beckham Jr.'s streak came to an end against the Carolina Panthers on Week 15 as he was held to only 76 yards. That was also when the first of his many infamous shenanigans occurred. He was involved in what was a very heated matchup with Panthers cornerback Josh Norman. It all started when there was a pre-game scuffle between Josh Norman and a Carolina Panthers player which irritated Odell Beckham Jr., who went on to lose his cool during the matchup with Norman.

The entire matchup between the two during the game was extremely physical. ODJ was flagged with three personal fouls while Norman had two. Beckham was so infuriated that he launched himself like a missile towards Norman's head with a helmet-to-helmet hit. It was a dangerous play on the part of Odell Jr., who was later suspended by the NFL for one game. Josh Norman called Odell Beckham Jr. an immature little kid because of what he was doing the entire game.[xv]

Odell Beckham Jr.'s season ended in the New York Giants' final game against the Philadelphia Eagles on January 3, 2016. He had 54 receiving yards in that game. But even though the season ended in another tough win-loss record for Beckham, the antics did not stop. This was when the world saw the controversial side of Odell Beckham Jr. as he exchanged tweets with Josh Norman on Twitter, a popular social media platform. It even came to the point where Beckham told Norman to be thankful to him for making him relevant, as the latter was not really known to be one of the better cornerbacks in the NFL.[xvi]

Nevertheless, even after his outrageous behavior, Odell Beckham Jr. was voted by his fellow players as tenth in the NFL Top 100 Players of 2016 thanks to his amazing performances in only his second year in the league. Making a second straight appearance in the Pro Bowl, Beckham finished his season with 96 receptions for 1450 yards and 13 touchdowns. There really was no sophomore slump for the rising NFL star, but he had begun to show the side of what was going to be one of the more interesting personalities the sporting world has seen in recent years.

The Rise to Stardom and the Antics Continued, First Playoff Appearance

After two unsuccessful regular-season campaigns for the New York Giants despite having had Odell Beckham Jr. in the lineup during both of those seasons, the franchise decided to go another direction by hiring new head coach Ben McAdoo to replace Tom Coughlin, who resigned from his position. Even with a new coach, Odell Beckham Jr. was still the center of the offense for the Giants. And the best part was, New York was finally going to be a contender with ODB in the lineup.

While it was no secret that Odell Beckham Jr. was always an animated person, it was during the 2016 season when the entire world witnessed the lengths he would go through to make it known that he was an entirely new breed of superstar in the world of the NFL. Hi status as a fan favorite only grew to legendary status while the rest of the league began telling him that there was no place for his brand of flair and personality.

In Week 1 of the 2016 season, Odell Beckham Jr. was instrumental in defeating the Dallas Cowboys on September 11, 2016. While he may have finished with 4 receptions for a total of 73 yards, it was his celebratory dance that caught the attention of the entire sporting world. At a time when the league was becoming more formal every season, the NFL thought that Beckham Jr.'s dance had no place in football and decided to fine him. A week later in a win over the Saints, he was once again fined by the league for a move that violated the safety protocols of the NFL.

After that win against the New Orleans Saints in Week 2, Odell Beckham Jr. entered Week 3 hoping to make a statement against the Washington Redskins, who had just recently acquired his rival, Josh Norman, after he was released by the Panthers. While Odell Jr. performed admirably by finishing the game with 7 receptions for 121 yards on his way to becoming the fastest player in league history to reach 200 receptions, the Giants ended up losing to the Redskins.

The frustrating performance that the Giants had against the Redskins made Beckham Jr. lose his cool. He threw a sideline tantrum, took his helmet off, and then slammed it into the kicking net. In turn, the kicking net fought back by bouncing Odell's helmet back towards his face. While the league saw how bad a scene it was whenever Beckham Jr. lost his cool, it was also the start of his somewhat weird yet special relationship with the kicking net.[xvi]

Opposing defenses began to notice how quickly Odell Beckham Jr. would allow his temper to get in the way of his game. In Week 4, the Minnesota Vikings' Xavier Rhodes defended Odell Jr. physically and essentially shut him down in what was eventually a very poor game for him. When Beckham felt that Rhodes was becoming too physical with him, he got into his defender's face and even bumped the official at one point. He got a fine and a loss in that lamentable 3-reception and 23-yard performance.

As the season steadily transpired, it was becoming clear to the New York Giants that they could only go as far as Odell Beckham Jr. could take them. When their star wide receiver was struggling, they were also struggling. This was true when Beckham was limited to 5 receptions and 56 yards against the Green Bay Packers in Week 5. But the opposite was also true. Whenever Beckham was in a winning state of mind, the New York Giants looked unstoppable.

In Week 6, Odell Beckham Jr. had one of the greatest games he had ever played at that point in his career when they went up against the Baltimore Ravens. He bounced back well after the two poor performances in the previous two weeks and went for 8 receptions for a new career-high of 222 yards and 2 touchdowns. Beckham Jr. also showcased one of the weirdest touchdown celebrations in league history when he proposed on bended knee to the kicking net after a 75-yard touchdown. He later claimed that the kicking net accepted his marriage proposal.[xvi]

From then on, the Giants won their next five games to go for a six-game winning streak, which ended on

December 4th against the Pittsburgh Steelers. He had a total of 7 touchdowns in those six straight wins. That included two 2-touchdown games in wins against the Philadelphia Eagles and the Cleveland Browns.

Coming into a match with the Philadelphia Eagles in Week 16 while leading the New York Giants to a 10-4 record, Odell Beckham Jr. was looking to push his team to a better record as he was eyeing the playoffs for the first time in his career. In that game, he did more than enough of what should have been necessary to help his team win that matchup. However, despite 11 receptions for 150 yards coming from Beckham, the Giants still fell short.

Odell Beckham Jr. was so upset about that loss that he let his emotions get the better of him once again. He was banging his head against a door just outside the visitors' locker room after losing that game against the Eagles. Several people from the Giants organization as well as some members of the media saw what had transpired as Odell Jr. was eventually escorted by team security inside the Giants' locker room to avoid escalating the scrutiny he was getting from the media.[xvi]

On January 1, 2017, the New York Giants defeated the Washington Redskins for their 11th win of the regular season. This allowed them to make it to the playoffs for the first time since 2011. In the middle of it all was Odell Beckham Jr., who upped his season totals to 101 receptions for 1367 yards and 10 touchdowns. It was the first time he started and played all 16 games of the season for the Giants while also making it to the playoffs for the first time in his rising career. Beckham Jr. also became a Pro Bowl selection for a third straight season and was voted by his fellow players as the eighth-best player in the NFL.

But while Odell Beckham Jr. was still productive as ever as a player on his way to leading his team to their most successful season in recent memory, the ongoing problem for the New York Giants was his temper. ODJ proved time and time again that he was a loose cannon that could suddenly go off at any given moment when he let his frustrations get the best of him, either due to a loss or because of a poor personal performance. The Giants loved having him around because of his stellar productivity as one of the best wide receivers in the entire league, but the issue for them was that they did not know what to expect of Odell Jr. when things did not go the way of their star player.

In that regard, there were also growing concerns about how truly selfless he was as a player. For one, even after winning a game against the Chicago Bears on November 20th, he was still visibly frustrated and even told the media that it was their defense that was bailing them out in crucial moments. He criticized his own team's offense and told them to step it up if they did not want the defense to be doing all the work for them all the time.

Beckham Jr. was indeed the biggest part of the Giants' offense, but he was just a receiver who had to rely on his other teammates to get him open for catches. And when he was asked by the media why he did not have the usual number of catches that game, he deflected the question by telling them to ask someone else, as he was possibly hinting that it was his teammates' fault for not getting him open or spotting him for what could have been target passes he would have caught.[xvii]

As undeniable as Odell Beckham Jr.'s talent was, there was also a belief that his "me first" mentality and his temper were canceling out what he was doing out there on the field. But the New York Giants needed to take the good with the bad because of how talented ODB truly was. The one thing they did not expect was for his temper to get the best of him in what was their most critical game since 2011.

In the New York Giants' playoff game against the Green Bay Packers on January 8th, Odell Beckham Jr.

got shut down by the defense and was left visibly frustrated in and off the pitch. The Giants ended up losing that game 13-38. This prompted one of the worst displays of frustration on the part of Odell Beckham Jr. The star wide receiver ended up punching a hole through the visitors' locker room wall of Lambeau Field. The Giants were quick to say that they were unaware of such an incident but were still going to pay for the damages.[xviii] While no one was hurt from that incident, what was clear was that Odell Beckham Jr. needed to work on how to control his temper and frustrations if he wanted to get to the next level as a superstar in the NFL.

The Injury Season

If there was something admirable about the New York Giants and their relationship with arguably their best player, it was that they always had Odell Beckham Jr.'s back and that they were willing to stick with him through thick and thin. This was evident when they decided to pick up and exercise the fifth year of his rookie contract entering the 2017 season despite all the temper tantrums and the frustrating moments he has had in his career. What anyone could possibly take from this transaction was that the Giants were banking on the possibility that Beckham Jr. would eventually learn how to control his emotions better as he matured together with the team.

Unfortunately for Odell Beckham Jr., things did not start off in the best of ways for him in what could have been a redemption season for the often-criticized star wide receiver. He had to miss the first week of his fourth season because of an ankle injury that would eventually hamper him throughout the rest of the season. Nevertheless, he still found the strength and perseverance to power through the injury and return to the lineup on Week 2.

In the Week 2 game against the Detroit Lions, Odell Beckham Jr. finished with 4 receptions for 36 yards in a loss. A week later, he had a better outing when he went for 9 yards receptions for 79 yards in a loss to the Philadelphia Eagles. He had 2 touchdowns in that game and once again showcased his love for dramatic flair when he had another one of those interestingly weird touchdown celebrations. Beckham pretended to be a dog and simulated the act of peeing in the end zone after scoring that touchdown. The act warranted him a penalty for what was considered unsportsmanlike conduct on his part.[xviii]

Odell Beckham Jr. continued to play well in the next two weeks for the New York Giants by going for a total of 12 receptions for 187 yards and a touchdown in losses to the Tampa Bay Buccaneers and the Los Angeles Chargers. But the sad part was that he ended up not playing one more game after that loss to the Chargers, wherein he had to leave early due to an injury.

The New York Giants later revealed that Odell Beckham Jr. suffered a fractured left ankle that required surgery to repair it. As such, he was out for the remainder of the season and was placed on injured reserve by the Giants. He was only able to play four games the entire season and had a total of 25 receptions for 302 yards and 3 touchdowns. For the rest of the season, fans and the league alike missed Odell Beckham Jr.'s brand of flamboyance and personality in both the positive and the negative senses.

The Return, Final Year with the Giants

Confident in their star player's health and knowing how stellar he had been for them ever since he entered the NFL back in 2014, the New York Giants decided to give Odell Beckham Jr. a five-year, $95 million contract extension. On his part, Odell Jr. promptly accepted the offer, which would have made the money he was making proportional to the productivity he had displayed since his rookie season.

Demonstrating his hunger to get back on the field after getting injured nearly a year ago, Odell Beckham Jr. went on to have 11 receptions for 111 yards in a loss to the Jacksonville Jaguars in his return game on September 9, 2018. On Week 3, he finished a win over the Houston Texans with 109 yards on 9 receptions. But it took him until Week 5 in a loss to the Carolina Panthers for him to score his first touchdown of the season. Proving that he was already fully healthy, OBJ finished that loss with 8 receptions for 131 yards and a single touchdown.

Odell Beckham Jr. took his sentiments and his feelings to the media following the frustrating losses to the Carolina Panthers and the Philadelphia Eagles. He was highly critical of his team's efforts as they were in the middle of a 1-5 start that season as well as under the team's third head coach in a span of only two seasons.

Beckham was essentially saying that his teammates needed to pick themselves up and start playing better without blaming anyone for their sorry start that season. But, then again, Odell Beckham Jr. also implied that he was not sure whether or not they could still win with quarterback Eli Manning calling plays.[xix]

In one interview, OBJ said that Eli Manning was still effective at throwing the ball but he also said that he thought that his quarterback was playing it safe by not allowing Beckham to use his explosive legs and quick bursts of speed to go over the top of the defense.[xx] He was visibly frustrated, not only about how he thought he was not getting enough catches at the best possible spots, but also about how the team was playing. This was beginning to spell doom for the outspoken star, even though Odell Beckham Jr. had just signed a lucrative five-year deal until 2023.

Odell Beckham's comments about quarterback Eli Manning drew the ire of head coach Pat Shurmur, who was reportedly so angry at his wide receiver that he wanted him to apologize for such statements. But, then again, ODB was always a man who stood by his own words and unique personality.[xxi] He did not regret saying or doing anything pertaining to his team because he regarded his statements and his actions as an "act of leadership" on his part.[xxii]

In terms of his style of leadership, Odell Beckham Jr. certainly had a lot of room left to grow. He was always vocal about how he felt about a certain situation or two and never regretted doing what he thought was right to help the team win games. His brand of leadership is as rare as his unique style on the field, and that certainly did not sit well with the New York Giants, as they thought that Beckham's comments were more harmful than helpful for the team as a whole. Regardless of what both ODB and the Giants believed, what was certain was that the star wide receiver was trying to shake the team up in any way he could to get something positive out of his teammates.

While Odell Beckham Jr.'s comments did not help the Giants that season as they continued to lose games, the star wide receiver was still trying his best to make something out of what was already becoming a lost season. In a loss to the Atlanta Falcons on October 22nd, OBJ had 8 receptions for 143 yards and a touchdown. In Week 8, he finished a loss to the Washington Redskins with 8 receptions for 136 yards. He then had 2 touchdowns against San Francisco in the team's second win through 10 weeks of NFL play. However, despite having a really bad season, Odell Beckham Jr. made history in Week 13 by throwing a 49-yard touchdown pass in a win over the Chicago Bears to not only prove that he is as capable as any other as a quarterback, but to also become the first non-quarterback player to have multiple touchdown passes in a single season since 2010. (He previously had a touchdown pass against the Carolina Panthers back in Week 5.)

Nonetheless, a quad injury kept Odell Beckham Jr. out of the active lineup for the rest of the season as he had played what was to be his final game for the New York Giants in that Week 13 win over the Chicago Bears. He finished the regular season playing 12 games and totaling for 77 receptions for 1052 yards and 6 touchdowns.

Those were not the numbers we were accustomed to when it came to Odell Beckham Jr.'s overall capabilities and talent level. But it was not as if he had slowed down. For many, it was clearly because of how the New York Giants were no longer built to allow Odell Beckham Jr. to wreak havoc out there on the pitch. In that case, an overhaul was needed. What no one at that time expected was that the Giants were willing to wave the white flag by deciding to get rid of their best offensive player in the last five seasons.

The Trade to the Cleveland Browns, A Fresh Start

The New York Giants finally decided to pull the plug on what seemed to be a dramatic and chaotic run with Odell Beckham Jr. even though they could not blame their lack of success on the man that had helped make them relevant in the past five seasons. On March 13, 2019, the Giants traded OBJ to the Cleveland Browns in a package that included Jabrill Peppers, Kevin Zeitler, and a 2019 first-round draft pick. The trade effectively ended Odell Jr.'s run with the Giants, who had taken him 12th overall back in the 2014 Draft without any expectations that he would become the star that he had turned out to be in such a short span of time.

On his part, Odell Beckham Jr. thought that the trade was too personal on the part of the Giants even though they had already stated that it had nothing to do with the star's personality and that the move was all about what they thought was best for the franchise business-wise and for them to move forward. Needless to say, Beckham Jr. felt like he was disrespected by the franchise when the Giants decided to trade him away to Cleveland.[xxiii]

But Odell Beckham Jr. still had some positives that he could take out from that trade to the Cleveland Browns. For one, it was a fresh start for him, as he now has a good opportunity to get away from the problems he saw were unresolvable back in New York. The new faces he would see on the field would allow him to take in a breath of fresh air while living a life that is entirely new and a bit different than the one he was used to back when he was in New York playing for the Giants. It was also a chance for him to silence the critics and naysayers that described him as someone who would give way to his emotions at any given time to the detriment of the team that he played for.

Another thing that Beckham Jr. was looking forward to in his move to the Cleveland Browns was that he was going to reunite with former LSU teammate Jarvis Landry. Back in college, Beckham teamed up with Landry to form what was arguably the deadliest duo of receivers in all of college football. Beckham already knew Landry as much as Landry already knew Beckham. In that sense, there was a lot of reason for both of these players to believe that the tandem pairing could perhaps become as special as it was back when they were still with the LSU Tigers. In a video interview together with his former teammate, OBJ even went so far as to say that the reunion with Jarvis Landry was a dream come true for him. Perhaps any LSU fan that followed these two players from 2011 to 2013 could also say that seeing them back together on the same team was a dream come true as well.

On September 8, 2019, Odell Beckham Jr. made his Cleveland Browns debut after missing the majority of training camp due to injury. In that game against the

Tennessee Titans, OBJ finished with 7 receptions for 71 yards in what was a tough loss. However, he was quick to bounce back in his second game with the Browns. In that 23-3 win over the New York Jets, he finished with 6 receptions for 161 yards and an 89-yard touchdown. He also wowed fans with the patented one-handed catch he made famous back when he was still with the LSU Tigers.

Although it was a relatively good start for Beckham in his first season with the Browns, he was quick to get himself in trouble when a tough defensive matchup against the Baltimore Ravens' Marlon Humphrey prompted a punch from the star wide receiver. In turn, Humphrey choked Beckham, to the dismay of head coach Freddie Kitchens, who thought that Humphrey should have been ejected following that dangerous attack on his star wide receiver.

In Week 6 of the 2019 NFL season, Odell Beckham Jr. broke the 100-yard mark for a second time when he finished a loss to the Seattle Seahawks with 6 receptions and 101 yards. But, as he was still adjusting to his new team while playing together with an equally adept receiver such as Jarvis Landry, he was not the statistically dominant player that he was in New York. For the majority of the season, OBJ was second to Landry in terms of receptions, receiving yards, and touchdowns as they were beginning to show the same dynamics that made them a duo that was feared all across America back when they were in LSU.

Chapter 5: Personal Life

Odell Beckham Jr. was born to athletic parents Odell Beckham Sr., a standout running back during his days at LSU, and Heather Van Norman, a track athlete back in her prime. Both of them met when they were still in LSU. While Odell Sr. never got to a more competitive playing field after college, Heather was able to take her talents to the national level. She was in the middle of training for the Olympics when she found out that she was pregnant with Odell Jr. She eventually went on to become the coach of the Nicholls State University track and field team after her days as an athlete.

Odell Sr. and Heather eventually separated when Beckham Jr. was still a child, but Heather got custody of the younger Odell and brought him to New Orleans to go to school to Newman during his fifth grade. However, the younger Odell still had a good relationship with his father, who taught him the basics of football and how to excel in sports. Odell Beckham Jr. also has a younger brother named Kordell and a younger sister named Jasmine.

Growing up, Odell Beckham Jr. was a fan of many sports. He played football, basketball, and track competitively. He was also a soccer player when he was a younger boy, but he had to quit because the training required him to spend some time overseas. He is still seen playing basketball from to time and can perform acrobatic dunks that not even guys who are six inches taller than him can pull off.

Odell Beckham Jr. is actually one of the more popular names, not only in the sporting world but also as a celebrity in his own right. He is known for his love of flair and for his unique fashion taste that has drawn the ire of the NFL due to how strict the league is in enforcing not only a code of conduct but also a dress code. Odell Jr. is also known for being a high-profile name in the world of endorsements as he has a huge contract with global sports giant Nike.

As a celebrity himself, Odell Beckham Jr. is no stranger to some of the biggest stars in the entire world. He is known to be good friends with pop icon Justin Bieber and was once seen together with the megastar at a party in Miami shortly after Odell and the New York Giants made the playoffs for the first time since 2011. Other than that, Beckham is also friends with basketball megastar LeBron James and retired soccer icon David Beckham, whom he idolized as a child.

While Odell Beckham Jr. can oftentimes be viewed by the media and the NFL negatively due to his unique blend of personality and on-the-field antics, he is one of the most charitable athletes in the world and has partnered with many charities that fund cancer research and other projects meant to help those displaced by floods and natural disasters. One of his most prominent acts of charity was when he pledged $500,000 from his jersey sales to help those affected by the flooding that happened in 2016 in his home state of Louisiana. He did this when he was still in the middle of his less-than-profitable rookie contract. He is also known for being active in partnering with the Make-A-Wish Foundation.

Chapter 6: Impact on Football, Legacy, and Future

If you mention the name of Odell Beckham Jr. to anyone who has a good working knowledge of the sporting world, he or she might be reminded of the play that catapulted the man into mega stardom as a rookie. It was that one-handed catch he made off of a throw from Eli Manning that turned a rising rookie into one of the most sensational athletes in all of sports. What really was so difficult about that touchdown catch was that Beckham, at only 5'11", was seemingly already out of balance and falling down on his back before he stretched his arms way back to the limit of his shoulders and then caught the ball with one hand in an instant.

In all of football, the one-handed catch is one of the more difficult plays to make because it is so hard to make the catch at full speed and against the pressure of the opposing defense. It is also very difficult to keep the ball safe in your hands right after making the catch. That is why coaches at the lowest levels of football will always teach kids to catch the ball with two hands as opposed to using only one hand. But Odell Beckham Jr. made the play look effortless even though it really was not.

With his back arched, his arm stretched back, and right foot off the ground to improve his reach, he was able to catch the ball while maintaining his balance for that touchdown. And, as the slow-motion cam revealed, he only needed three fingers to make the catch. This brought the entire world into a frenzy as they were able to witness what is arguably the greatest catch ever made in the history of football.

In the world of football, the first catch to be recorded happened in 1906. As iconic as the first catch was, there really was nothing more spectacular than what Odell Beckham Jr. did using his athleticism, long arms, and large and strong fingers to perform that one-handed catch. Since that time, every catch that has ever been made at any level of football has always been compared to the one that Beckham Jr. performed. In short, Beckham Jr.'s one-handed catch has become the standard for any flashy catch.

The impact that this catch has had on the world of football has inspired younger players to practice the one-handed catch even though coaches in the past did not like it when their players caught the ball with one hand instead of two. Think of it this way—during the 90s and the 2000s, basketball coaches would scold players who pull up from the three-point line as their first option on offense. That is because the three-point shot was considered inefficient at a time when players were not yet skilled enough to hit it with consistency. Moreover, a longer shot like the three-pointer usually leads to long rebounds that are difficult to grab for offensive players. As such, those shots were considered "one-and-dones" when they are not making it through the hoop and are very risky for any team or player to take.

However, ever since players like Stephen Curry exploded onto the scene to hit dribble pull-up three-point shots with ease while also winning games, and ever since advanced statistics showed how truly efficient the shot is, the first option on offense for a lot of NBA teams today is now the three-pointer. To that end, players are now shooting more than ten three-pointers on average as compared to a time when the best three-point shooters back in the 90s and 2000s were barely taking more than five three-pointers in a game. What used to be a bad play has become a go-to shot in today's basketball.

The same could be said of the one-handed catch. Thanks to how Odell Beckham Jr. made the catch so popular with that phenomenal play he had against the Dallas Cowboys in 2014, players are now performing the catch on a regular basis. The one-handed catch has been the gold standard for many receivers not because it adds extra points like the three-pointer does, but because it fires up the team and the crowd and also allows the player some extra inches to stretch out his hand for a catch that would have been impossible had it been done using two hands.

Today, younger players are now practicing the play the same way Odell Beckham Jr. did when he was still in high school and in college. He has allowed the receiver position to evolve into a role that could fire up the crowd and make headlines the same way he did when he became one of football's biggest stars just by performing a catch that only he could make.

When you look at what Odell Beckham Jr. has done as a football player, he really is not the most well-decorated athlete in that regard because he still lacks the wins and the major awards that will allow him to make the claim that he is one of the greatest to have ever played the game. However, his legacy will always be measured by how much he changed the wide receiver position by making the one-handed catch a routine play, the same way Stephen Curry and James Harden made the three-point shot the deadliest go-to weapon in basketball.

While Odell Beckham Jr. lacks the accolades and the championships that most other football superstars have under their belts, he can still argue himself to be the sport's biggest star today, not because of his stats or his achievements but simply because of his star power and how he affects the sport on and off the field. He is the LeBron James of football due to his influence and his ability to pull people over to his side. Players such as Drew Brees, DeAndre Hopkins, Mike Evans, Tom Brady, Antonio Brown, and Aaron Rodgers may end up having more successful careers in terms of statistics and wins but, right now, football's most recognizable player is Odell Beckham Jr.

No, it is not only about Beckham's all-time great catch. There are actually a lot of reasons why he is considered the most iconic player of his generation.[xxiv] First off, at a time when the NFL strictly polices the way their players dress, Odell Jr. has become a rebel with his own unique style. He consistently wears customized cleats with color designs that border illegality as far as the NFL is concerned. Idolizing the Joker, the polarizing villain from the comic book *The Batman*, ODJ had the character on his visor and once wore shoes that resembled the Joker's colors, which drew the ire of the NFL. Off the field, he is known for his own unique fashion sense and for his amazing sense of style. And no one can ever deny that his signature hairstyle, that bleached blonde hair, is one of the more recognizable looks in all of sports.

Moreover, Odell Beckham Jr. also wears that star-like aura and owns up to his status as a megastar at a time when the NFL prefers football players to be more or less discreet about their business. He is often seen at the most important events celebrities usually attend. One of the cases that can be pointed out was when he was present at the third meeting between the Golden State Warriors and the Cleveland Cavaliers in the NBA Finals. Another noteworthy moment was when he partied with Justin Bieber in Miami. He simply is the star that fits this generation of young people but is the star that the NFL would not prefer to be the one carrying the league's banner due to his polarizing personality and flair.

And when it comes to what he does on the playing field, no other player can get a crowd roaring more than Odell Beckham Jr. can. He routinely performs one-handed catches and has a knack for celebrating in the most entertaining of ways such as when he proposed to the kicking net after a touchdown. No one on the field has more fun than Beckham does, and no one is as entertaining to the people as he is.

All that being said, ODJ has become someone whose star has transcended football. He is now more than just a football player to the eyes of many people around the world. He is effectively a celebrity whose status is hardly affected by his poor in-game performances and his lack of success on the field. He is a generational icon, not just because of his talent but also because of his overall personality. Odell Beckham Jr. is the star that the NFL needs to make the sport "fun" again and is also the kind of personality that can keep people glued to their television sets regardless of whether or not he is doing something that is football-related.

As a football player, his status as one of the greats may be questioned by his lack of wins and individual accolades but he will always be regarded as one of the biggest icons the sport has ever seen. A championship or even a few more playoff appearances might solidify his spot as one of the best players of his generation, but he will always be regarded as someone who brought his own brand of showmanship and noteworthy moments to the sport.

Final Word/About the Author

I was born and raised in Norwalk, Connecticut. Growing up, I could often be found spending many nights watching basketball, soccer, and football matches with my father in the family living room. I love sports and everything that sports can embody. I believe that sports are one of most genuine forms of competition, heart, and determination. I write my works to learn more about influential athletes in the hopes that from my writing, you the reader can walk away inspired to put in an equal if not greater amount of hard work and perseverance to pursue your goals. If you enjoyed *Odell Beckham Jr.: The Inspiring Story of One of Football's Greatest Wide Receivers,* please leave a review! Also, you can read more of my works on *Serena Williams, Rafael Nadal, Roger Federer, Novak Djokovic, Richard Sherman, Andrew Luck, Rob Gronkowski, Brett Favre, Calvin Johnson, Drew Brees, J.J. Watt, Colin Kaepernick, Aaron Rodgers, Peyton Manning, Tom Brady, Russell Wilson, Gregg*

Popovich, Pat Riley, John Wooden, Steve Kerr, Brad Stevens, Red Auerbach, Doc Rivers, Erik Spoelstra, Michael Jordan, LeBron James, Kyrie Irving, Klay Thompson, Stephen Curry, Kevin Durant, Russell Westbrook, Anthony Davis, Chris Paul, Blake Griffin, Kobe Bryant, Joakim Noah, Scottie Pippen, Carmelo Anthony, Kevin Love, Grant Hill, Tracy McGrady, Vince Carter, Patrick Ewing, Karl Malone, Tony Parker, Allen Iverson, Hakeem Olajuwon, Reggie Miller, Michael Carter-Williams, John Wall, James Harden, Tim Duncan, Steve Nash, Draymond Green, Kawhi Leonard, Dwyane Wade, Ray Allen, Pau Gasol, Dirk Nowitzki, Jimmy Butler, Paul Pierce, Manu Ginobili, Pete Maravich, Larry Bird, Kyle Lowry, Jason Kidd, David Robinson, LaMarcus Aldridge, Derrick Rose, Paul George, Kevin Garnett, Chris Paul, Marc Gasol, Yao Ming, Al Horford, Amar'e Stoudemire, DeMar DeRozan, Isaiah Thomas, Kemba Walker, Chris Bosh, Andre Drummond, JJ Redick, DeMarcus Cousins, Wilt Chamberlain, Bradley Beal,

Rudy Gobert, Aaron Gordon, Kristaps Porzingis, Nikola Vucevic, Andre Iguodala, Devin Booker, John Stockton, Jeremy Lin, Chris Paul, Pascal Siakam, Jayson Tatum, Gordon Hayward, Nikola Jokic, Bill Russell, Victor Oladipo, Luka Doncic, Ben Simmons, Shaquille O'Neal, Joel Embiid, Donovan Mitchell, Damian Lillard and Giannis Antetokounmpo in the Kindle Store. If you love football, check out my website at claytongeoffreys.com to join my exclusive list where I let you know about my latest books and give you lots of goodies.

Like what you read? Please leave a review!

I write because I love sharing the stories of influential athletes like Odell Beckham Jr. with fantastic readers like you. My readers inspire me to write more so please do not hesitate to let me know what you thought by leaving a review! If you love books on life, sports, or productivity, check out my website at claytongeoffreys.com to join my exclusive list where I let you know about my latest books. Aside from being the first to hear about my latest releases, you can also download a free copy of *33 Life Lessons: Success Principles, Career Advice & Habits of Successful People*. See you there!

Clayton

References

[i] Casey, Connor. "Odell Beckham Jr. claim's his dad and Shaq were roommates in LSU". *247 Sports*. 18 September 2018. Web.

[ii] Graziano, Dan. "Odell Beckham Jr. discusses meeting David Beckham, controlling emotions on field". *ABC News*. 23 April 2015. Web.

[iii] Elsen, Michael. "Odell Beckham Jr. meets idol David Beckham". *Giants.com*. 27 April 2015. Web.

[iv] O'Connor, Ian. "Behind Odell Beckham Jr.'s quest for greatness". *ESPN*. 18 December 2015. Web.

[v] Armstrong, Kevin. "The rise of NY Giants wide receiver Odell Beckham Jr.". *New York Daily News*. 6 December 2014. Web.

[vi] Sobleski, Brent. "Looking Back at the High School Scouting Reports of Today's Biggest NFL Stars". *Bleacher Report*. Web.

[vii] Kerr-Dineen, Luke. "Five years ago, Odell Beckham Jr. made the most modest Signing Day interview". *For the Win*. 3 February 2016. Web.

[viii] Hickey, Kevin. "Les Miles to Giants' Odell Beckham Jr.: Eliminate 'social pressure'". *USA Today*. 11 January 2017. Web.

[ix] Petrak, Scott. "Les Miles believes Odell Beckham Jr. will be happy with Browns, do great things reunited with Jarvis Landry". *Browns Zone*. 25 March 2019. Web.

[x] McCrystal, Ryan. "Odell Beckham Jr. NFL Draft 2014: Highlights, Scouting Report for Giants WR". *Bleacher Report*. 4 February 2014. Web.

[xi] Kadar, Dan. "Odell Beckham Jr. 2014 NFL Draft scouting report". *SB Nation*. 21 April 2014. Web.

[xii] Fahey, Cian. "Odell Beckham Jr. Is Definition of Special Talent with Rookie Domination". *Bleacher Report*. 26 December 2014. Web.

[xiii] "Odell Beckham's one-handed grab might be the best catch of the year". *Fox Sports*. 23 November 2014. Web.

[xiv] "Odell Beckham Jr. named offensive rookie of the month". *Giants.com*. 4 December 2014. Web.

[xv] Reyes, Lorenzo. "A brief history of the Josh Norman-Odell

Beckham Jr. feud". *USA Today*. 21 September 2016. Web.

[xvi] Raanan, Jordan. "A timeline of OBJ's shenanigans". *ESPN*. 26 September 2017. Web.

[xvii] Glauber, Bob. "Odell Beckham Jr.'s temper an ongoing concern for Giants". *Newsday*. 23 November 2016. Web.

[xviii] Raanan, Jordan. "Odell Beckham Jr. bangs head on door, allegedly punches hole in wall". *ESPN*. 9 January 2017. Web.

[xix] Vacchiano, Ralph. "Odell Beckham Jr.'s Giant message seems clear: Eli Manning isn't the quarterback he wants". *SNY.com*. 19 October 2018. Web.

[xx] Schonbrun, Zach. "The Once-Boring Giants Now Have a Drama Problem". *New York Times*. 10 October 2018. Web.

[xxi] Gibbs, Dan. "Odell Beckham Jr controversy: 'LIVID' New York Giants coach forces star to apologise". *Express*. 12 October 2018. Web.

[xxii] Lombardo, Matt. "Giants' Odell Beckham Jr. believes his controversial comments were leadership moment ... were they?". *NJ.com*. 29 January 2019. Web.

[xxiii] Bumbaca, Chris. "Cleveland Browns' Odell Beckham Jr. on trade: Giants 'thought they'd send me here to die'". *USA Today*. 20 August 2019. Web.

[xxiv] Lyles, Harry Jr. "Odell Beckham Jr. will be the most iconic player of his generation". *SB Nation*. 10 July 2017. Web.

Made in the USA
Columbia, SC
20 June 2022

61960715R00063